The Joy of Ballet Music

Thirty-seven best loved themes from famous ballets and ballet scenes from operas. Selected and arranged for piano solo by Denes Agay.

Foreword

For the past few decades, in America and many other countries of the world, ballet has been enjoying an unprecedented and ever increasing popularity. Never throughout history has it attracted such wide and enthusiastic audiences. The purpose of this folio is to present, in one volume, the best-loved selections of every type of ballet, including ballet scenes from operas.

The piano arrangements, expertly fashioned by Denes Agay with his well-known skill and taste, are in the easy-to-intermediate levels, well within the capabilities of pianists of modest technical attainments.

We hope that not only the great number of ballet enthusiasts but the entire music loving public will enjoy playing and listening to these selections that range from the early Romantic era to the favorites of the Modern repertory.

The Publishers

Order No. YK 21350
US International Standard Book Number: 978.0.8256.8035.9
UK International Standard Book Number: 0.7119.0706.4

Yorktown Music Press, Inc.

DISTRIBUTED BY

Dance of the Sugar Plum Fairy

Theme from The Nutcracker

Peter I. Tchaikovsky

Andante con moto

Russian Dance

from The Nutcracker

Peter I. Tchaikovsky

Waltz of the Flowers

from The Nutcracker

Peter I. Tchaikovsky

8

Sheherazade

from The Young Prince and The Young Princess

Nikolai Rimsky-Korsakov

Mazurka

from Coppelia

Leo Delibes

Czardas

from Coppelia

Leo Delibes

Valse Lente

from Coppelia

Leo Delibes

Tempo di Valse moderato

The Sleeping Beauty Waltz

from Aurora's Wedding

Peter I. Tchaikovsky

The Rose Adagio

from The Sleeping Beauty

Peter I. Tchaikovsky

Scene from *Swan Lake*

Peter I. Tchaikovsky

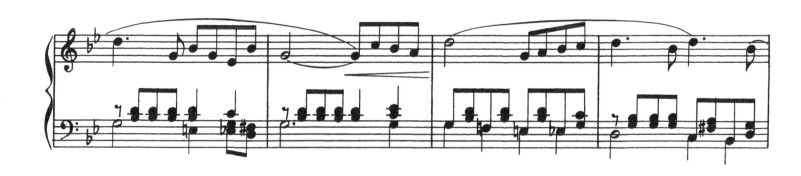

Dance of the Little Swans

from Swan Lake

Peter I. Tchaikovsky

Pas de Deux

from Giselle

Adolphe Adam

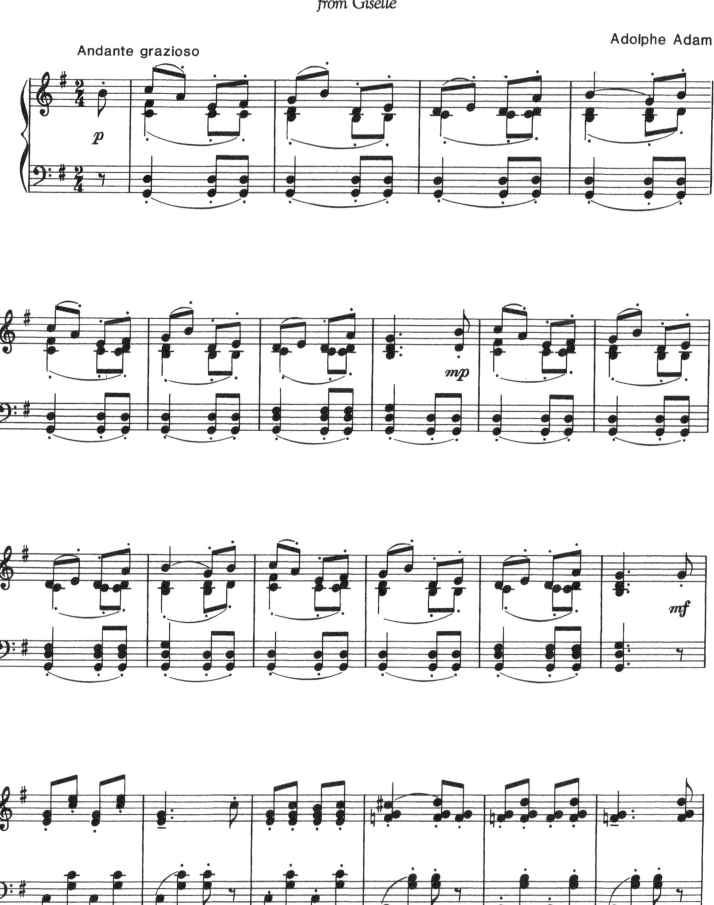

Grand Valse

excerpt from Giselle

Adolphe Adam

Pas de Fleurs

from Naila

Leo Delibes

Scene from *Bluebeard*

Jacques Offenbach

35

Russian Sailors' Dance

from The Red Poppy

Reinhold Glière

Hesitation Waltz

from The Red Poppy

Reinhold Glière

Slow languorous waltz tempo

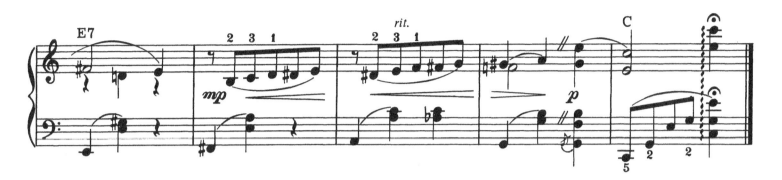

Prelude

from Les Sylphides

Frederic Chopin

(In the ballet, this *Prelude* is played
successively three times: *mf, p, pp*.)

Nocturne

from Les Sylphides

Frederic Chopin

Saber Dance

from Gayne

Aram Khatchaturian

Theme from *Prince Igor*

Alexander Borodin

Polovetzian Dance

from Prince Igor

Alexander Borodin

Can-Can

from La Vie Parisienne

Jacques Offenbach

Pizzicato Polka

from Sylvia

Leo Delibes

Aragonaise

from Le Cid

Jules Massenet

Dance of the Hours

from La Gioconda

Amilcare Ponchielli

Allegro

Mirror Dance

from Faust

Charles Gounod

61

Danse Antique

from Faust

Charles Gounod

63

Dance of the Priestesses

from Aida

Giuseppe Verdi

Dance of the Princess

from The Firebird

Igor Stravinsky

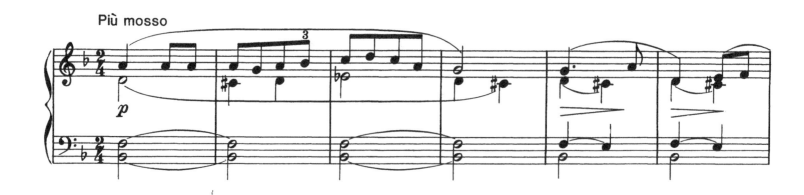

Finale from *The Firebird*

Igor Stravinsky

Pas de Six

from William Tell

Gioacchino Rossini

Polka from *The Golden Age*

Dmitri Shostakovich

Folk Dance

from Romeo and Juliet

Serge Prokofieff

Bacchanale

from Samson and Delilah

Camille Saint-Saens

Valse Grotesque

from Petroushka

Igor Stravinsky

Dance of the Ballerina

from Petroushka

Igor Stravinsky